PROVERBS 31
in 5 Minutes a Day

Proverbs 31

IN 5 MINUTES A DAY

A Bible Study for Women

MARI HERNANDEZ-TUTEN

Illustration by Chrissy Lau

ROCKRIDGE
PRESS

For general information on our other products and services or to obtain technical sup-port, please contact our Customer Care Department within the United States at (866) 744-2665, or outside the United States at (510) 253-0500.

Rockridge Press publishes its books in a variety of electronic and print formats. Some content that appears in print may not be available in electronic books, and vice versa.

TRADEMARKS: Rockridge Press and the Rockridge Press logo are trademarks or reg-istered trademarks of Callisto Media Inc. and/or its affiliates, in the United States and other countries, and may not be used without written permission. All other trademarks are the property of their respective owners. Rockridge Press is not associated with any product or vendor mentioned in this book.

All Scripture quotations, unless otherwise indicated, are taken from THE HOLY BIBLE, NEW INTERNATIONAL VERSION®, NIV® Copyright © 1973, 1978, 2011 by Biblica, Inc.® Used by permission. All rights reserved worldwide. Scripture quotations marked ESV are from the ESV® Bible (The Holy Bible, English Standard Version®), copyright © 2001 by Crossway Bibles, a publishing ministry of Good News Publishers. Used by permis-sion. All rights reserved. Scripture quotations marked (KJV) are taken from the King James Version of the Bible. Public domain.

Interior and Cover Designer: Mando Daniel
Photo Art Director/Art Manager: Tom Hood
Editor: Lauren O'Neal
Illustrations © Chrissy Lau 2020

ISBN: Print 978-1-64739-670-1 | eBook 978-1-64876-901-6

R1

For my mom and dad, who gave me the most precious gift of all: Jesus. You've left a legacy of faith that I pray will be deeply rooted and grounded as we live out His truth for generations to come.

Table of Contents

Introduction

One of the most misunderstood women in the Bible is the Proverbs 31 woman. The passage that describes her, Proverbs 31:10–31, is often mistaken for an overwhelming list of requirements for the Christian woman. For much of my life, I avoided Proverbs 31 because, after studying it, I felt "less than" or like I wasn't doing enough. You see, I was reading it like a job description, as if I had to have all the listed requirements and extensive experience in order to apply for God's love.

But what if there's a different way to look at it? What if it's a reflection of who we are when we're standing at the foot of the cross? Maybe, just maybe, it's who we become when we are gazing at God and "being transformed into his image with ever-increasing glory" (2 Corinthians 3:18).

I've been in ministry for more than 20 years, sharing God's truth and hope with women through mentoring, Bible teaching, family life coaching, and workshops. I've seen over and over again how comparison robs our joy, how we hustle to gain our worth, and how we live in fear that we aren't doing enough. I've written this book to remind our forgetful hearts that God loves us and we have influence right where He has us.

Remember Jesus's baptism in Mark 1:11? The voice of God tears open the heavens, and the most powerful and loving words echo from above: "You are my Son, whom I love; with you I am well pleased." This happened before Jesus began His ministry. He had not performed miraculous healings, raised people from the dead, or cast out demons. Those words were a Father's blessing to His Son. And these are the words of our Heavenly Father to you as you begin this Bible study journey: "You are My beloved. You are My daughter. I am pleased."

My prayer is that as we study together over the next seven weeks, you will see the character of God woven into each word of Proverbs 31 and see a reflection of who you are when you fix your gaze on Him. May you hear your proud Father speak these words over you, His daughter: "You are beloved." Not because of what you've done, but because of what Jesus has done on the cross and is doing through you. Live loved.

How to Use This Book

What Is Proverbs 31?

Proverbs 31—or, more specifically, Proverbs 31:10–31—is a poem in the book of Proverbs that describes a godly woman. Often, reading this passage feels like scrolling through a perfect friend's social media feed. It can leave you feeling overwhelmed, overworked, and overweight. Okay, maybe not overweight—but you may wonder how you missed the memo that purple is the new black and spindling is all the rage.

But when you really dig into this passage, you find that there's so much more to it. It's not obvious in the English translation, but in the original Hebrew, Proverbs 31:10–31 is an acrostic poem. Each line begins with a different letter of the Hebrew alphabet, starting with the first letter (*aleph*) and ending with the last (*tav*). "This is helpful to know," says John Piper in a sermon on the subject, "because it tips us off that the author is not building an argument like Paul does in Romans. Instead, he is stringing pearls."

Proverbs 31:10–31 is not about a specific woman who "has it all." It's more like a character sketch of who God has created us to be as we serve Him in our families and communities. It doesn't demand perfection from us; it shows us how perfect God is. That's what we'll discover and explore together over the course of this Bible study.

What's in This Book?

Every week, for seven weeks, we'll focus on a different part of Proverbs 31 until we've covered all the verses in order. You'll find commentary, study questions, journal prompts, and more—something for every day of each week. It's designed for the busy woman who wants to dive into God's Word, so each day will require only about five minutes of your time—except the seventh day of each week, which offers a longer study session so you can delve in and really absorb what you've learned, either on your own or as part of a group.

When and How to Read

Because this study only takes five minutes a day, you can fit it into your schedule in whatever way works best for you. You might make a daily habit of reading it in the morning with a cup of tea or at night before bed, or you might squeeze it in while on your lunch break or waiting in the car for your kids to finish soccer practice. Likewise, you can work through this book on your own, with a group at church, or with just a few friends or family members. There's no wrong way to spend time in the Word.

Necessary Materials

You'll be working straight out of this book. Grab a pen or pencil and your Bible (an app or audio version is fine!).

You Can Do It!

If you fall behind on some days, don't beat yourself up—you can always catch up the next day. Whether you find Proverbs 31 intimidating, inspiring, or a completely new experience, ask God to give you a fresh perspective and a deeper love for Him as we study this passage over the next seven weeks. You don't want to miss any of what you can glean about who God is and who you are, not only as a woman but also as a daughter of the King.

Proverbs 31:10–31

¹⁰ *A wife of noble character who can find?*
She is worth far more than rubies.
¹¹ *Her husband has full confidence in her*
and lacks nothing of value.
¹² *She brings him good, not harm,*
all the days of her life.
¹³ *She selects wool and flax*
and works with eager hands.
¹⁴ *She is like the merchant ships,*
bringing her food from afar.
¹⁵ *She gets up while it is still night;*
she provides food for her family
and portions for her female servants.
¹⁶ *She considers a field and buys it;*
out of her earnings she plants a vineyard.
¹⁷ *She sets about her work vigorously;*
her arms are strong for her tasks.
¹⁸ *She sees that her trading is profitable,*
and her lamp does not go out at night.
¹⁹ *In her hand she holds the distaff*
and grasps the spindle with her fingers.
²⁰ *She opens her arms to the poor*
and extends her hands to the needy.
²¹ *When it snows, she has no fear for*
her household;

for all of them are clothed in scarlet.
²² *She makes coverings for her bed;*
she is clothed in fine linen and purple.
²³ *Her husband is respected at the city gate,*
where he takes his seat among the elders
of the land.
²⁴ *She makes linen garments and sells them,*
and supplies the merchants with sashes.
²⁵ *She is clothed with strength and dignity;*
she can laugh at the days to come.
²⁶ *She speaks with wisdom,*
and faithful instruction is on her tongue.
²⁷ *She watches over the affairs of her household*
and does not eat the bread of idleness.
²⁸ *Her children arise and call her blessed;*
her husband also, and he praises her:
²⁹ *"Many women do noble things,*
but you surpass them all."
³⁰ *Charm is deceptive, and beauty is fleeting;*
but a woman who fears the Lord is
to be praised.
³¹ *Honor her for all that her hands have done,*
and let her works bring her praise at
the city gate.

Week One

A wife of noble character who can find?
She is worth far more than rubies.
Her husband has full confidence in her
and lacks nothing of value.
She brings him good, not harm,
all the days of her life.

PROVERBS 31:10–12

Day 1

Let's start this journey by making one thing clear: Proverbs 31 is not a job description or a checklist that earns you God's approval, love, or salvation once you complete it. It's a passage reminding us of who we are in Him. Our works, talents, successes, and "good girl" status do not save us. Only by His great mercy and the redeeming work of Jesus Christ are we saved. Proverbs 31 is about the woman you are and can be in Christ and only in Christ.

This passage is much like a parent telling a child as they leave home, "Remember who you are and whose you are." Remembering whose we are is what gives us the courage to be who we are. You are a daughter of the King—an *eshet chayil*, in Hebrew. Don't worry, it's a compliment. For now, you'll have to take my word for it, but we'll discuss this in depth over the next few days.

Because of the cross, we can walk in courage, not fear. In Him, we can be strong, not weak. In Romans 8:37, Paul writes, "We are more than conquerors." How? "Through Him who loved us." You see, even though our good works, skills, and gifts matter, they're not what give us victory and strength. God gives us conquering strength and victory through the power of the Holy Spirit because He loves us. Let's lean into Him!

You can and should live a life of "noble character" through the power of the Holy Spirit, but it does not earn you salvation and it does not make you more lovable. It has taken me years to understand this, and with each passing day, moment, and opportunity, I have to choose to believe it.

Because He is our Savior, we can live and serve Him freely, not in bondage to a "hustle hard" lifestyle. "For it is by grace you have been saved, through faith—and this is not from yourselves, it is the gift of God" (Ephesians 2:8). That word, "gift," means you don't work for it; you simply receive His saving grace. Because our hope is in our Savior, not our works, we can courageously walk in freedom as daughters of the King.

In what ways are you relying on His saving work, and in what ways are you still relying on your working hands?

_____

_____

_____

_____

_____

_____

_____

_____

_____

_____

_____

_____

_____

_____

_____

_____

Day 2

In the original Hebrew, Proverbs 31:10 starts with the words *eshet chayil. Eshet* is a form of the word *ishah,* which is Hebrew for both "woman" and "wife." *Chayil* can be translated as "virtuous" (KJV), "excellent" (ESV), or "noble" (NIV), but in most of the Old Testament, it's used to describe courageous, capable warriors. So let's translate *eshet chayil* as "woman of valor."

We are women of valor because God is in us. We are women of noble character, courage, and strength because our hope is in our Savior. You, my sister, have influence right where God has planted you, and don't let the enemy tell you any different.

Not only do you have influence—you are also valuable. The second sentence of Proverbs 31:10 says, "She is far more precious than jewels" (ESV) or "She is worth far more than rubies" (NIV). Regardless of the translation, the point is made: You are valuable. Not because you have a high-powered career, because you homeschool your kids, or because you live in a nice house, but because you are made in God's image.

Friends, let us boldly proclaim this God-given identity as we confidently stand in His truth and lean into His Spirit for wisdom. Let us be women on a mission, ready and audacious, willing to face each task and trial set before us because we know God is on our side.

Today, take a few moments to reflect on the women of valor God has placed in your life and stop to thank God for two of them by name.

Day 3

What about Proverbs 31 gives you clues that this is not one day in the life of a woman but rather various seasons in a woman's life? There's no right or wrong answer. To get you started, look at verse 12. It says, "all the days of her life."

_____

_____

_____

_____

_____

_____

_____

_____

_____

Where in this poem do you see life-giving words that celebrate courageous women who are clothed with strength, dignity, and trust in God? What character traits do you see in yourself from this passage? Again, there are no right or wrong answers.

_____

_____

_____

_____

_____

_____

_____

_____

_____

Day 4

It can happen to any of us. With each article we peruse, each message we read, and each social media update we receive, the lie gets louder in our heads: "You have nothing to offer." I've fallen victim to this idea myself. How many times have you canceled or ignored an outing, opportunity, or activity because you believed the lie that you have nothing to offer? The messages that echo in your heart may come from lies you believe, labels you've been given, or your past mistakes or sins. In instances like these, you need to remind your heart that there's no need to feel fear or paralysis because you don't earn God's love through your actions. His love is a gift that has already been given to us at the cross.

These lies haunt us as women no matter what season of life we're in, but Proverbs 31 lets us know that when God sees you, He sees a daughter of the King, made in His image, who's been redeemed and is "worth far more than rubies." Jesus's saving work on the cross is what makes you worthy!

When we're gripped by the lies and paralyzed by the fear, we put on the belt of truth and ask the Holy Spirit to give us wisdom to discern what is true. Let's learn to distinguish between God's words and Satan's words so we can make sure we are listening to the correct voice.

How Satan Speaks

Condemns

Shames

Mean

Frightening

Hateful

How God Speaks

Convicts

Loves

Kind

Comforting

Encouraging

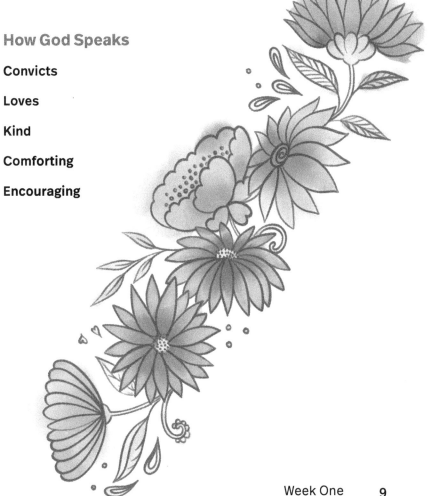

It is important not only to label the lies for what they are but also to replace them with God's truth. For each lie that follows, look up the corresponding verse in the "Truths" column and write down the truth you glean from the verse.

Lies

1. God will never forgive me.

2. God can't use me because of my past mistakes.

3. This situation will defeat me.

4. God has abandoned me.

5. God can't be trusted.

Truths

1. **1 John 1:9** He is faithful and just to forgive us.

2. **2 Corinthians 5:17** _____

3. **Romans 8:37** _____

4. **Psalm 46:1** _____

5. **Hebrews 10:23** _____

At times like this, we need to cling to God's truth and remember who we are in light of it. Let putting your hope in our Savior give you courage this week to fight against any lies and fears that enter your mind!

Day 5

In his book *The 7 Habits of Highly Effective People*, Stephen Covey talks about what he calls our "circle of influence." We may think we don't have influence because we've been believing the lie that we're "just" a wife, nurse, teacher, mom, cashier, grandma. But the reality is that we influence others every day, no matter what hat we're wearing. Proverbs 31 is all about a woman using what God has given her to glorify Him where she has influence—within her family and her community.

Covey talks about what happens when our "circle of concern" becomes bigger than our circle of influence. When we're gripped by fear and lies, we waste our time and energy on things we can't do anything about. As a result, God gets smaller in our heads, our abilities seem useless, and our influence on the world around us decreases. That's exactly where the enemy wants us: defeated, with decreased influence for the Kingdom of God.

Now let's consider our circles of influence. Look at the following image. The dot in the middle is you. In the circle right around you, your center circle, are the people closest to you, like your immediate family and close friends. In the next circle out, your inner circle, are people you know fairly well—perhaps coworkers, neighbors, and members of your church. Finally, the last circle, the outer circle, contains people you know but not very well, like casual acquaintances and distant family members. Jot down a few names in each circle.

Outer Circle

Inner Circle

Center Circle

How do you influence the people in your center circle? Inner circle? Outer circle? Is it a positive influence or a negative influence? Where and how can you have the greatest impact?

_____

_____

_____

_____

_____

_____

_____

_____

_____

Pray for those in your center circle and ask God to help you influence them for His glory.

Day 6

Never underestimate what Christ did for us through the Cross. By it our salvation was won, and by it our lives—and our world—can be transformed. What difference does the Cross make in your life?

—BILLY GRAHAM

Guided Prayer

Heavenly Father, amazing things happen when we become women who have scripture deeply ingrained in our hearts and live it out within our sphere of influence through the power of the Holy Spirit. Open the eyes of my heart so I can see that Your grace is enough for me. Help me stop pursuing performance and instead pursue the person of Christ with courage and resolve. I want to be audacious and willing to allow your transforming work to move in my heart as I study Proverbs 31. Amen.

Day 7

Congratulations, you made it through your first week of study! We'll take the seventh day as an opportunity to delve in and spend more time than usual with Proverbs 31 by reviewing, discussing, and taking action.

Review

Here's what we talked about this week.

→ Proverbs 31 is like snapshots showing how a woman of noble character lives her life in the context of her family and community—*not* a checklist of tasks you have to accomplish in order to earn God's love.

→ This poem is much like a parent telling their child as they leave home, "Remember who you are and whose you are."

→ The Hebrew phrase *eshet chayil* can be translated as "woman of valor." The word *chayil* can mean virtuous, noble, courageous, or strong. This word is often used in the Old Testament to refer to valiant warriors. The cross makes us women of valor!

→ When we are gripped by fear and lies, we waste our time and energy on things we can't do anything about. In turn, our God gets smaller in our heads, our abilities seem useless, and our influence decreases. When we recall that He has a purpose for us right here where He has us, we can have a greater impact on our circle of influence as we serve the Lord.

Discuss

Answer these questions on your own or in a group.

1. What surprised you most about this week's lessons?

_____

_____

_____

_____

_____

_____

_____

_____

_____

_____

2. How does it make you feel, knowing that the Creator of the whole earth thinks you're more precious than jewels?

_____

_____

_____

_____

_____

_____

_____

_____

_____

_____

3. What was one situation in the past week in which you had to remind yourself that He is your Savior, not you?

_____

_____

_____

_____

_____

_____

_____

_____

4. What are some different ways you can live out your faith as a woman, friend, wife, mom, daughter, coworker, boss, and so on?

_____

_____

_____

_____

_____

_____

_____

_____

_____

_____

5. What from this week challenged you?

_____

_____

_____

_____

_____

_____

_____

_____

_____

Act

Here are some things you can do in the next week to put the lessons you've learned into action.

→ Write down the following words on an index card and put it where you will see it often: "You are a chosen people ... God's special possession, that you may declare the praises of him who called you out of the darkness into the light" (1 Peter 2:9).

→ Celebrate the courageous women in your life. Send a message to at least two women of valor you know, telling them how they've been examples of wisdom and strength in your life.

→ There is great freedom in accepting the gift of salvation God has given you. If you haven't already prayed the salvation prayer, I encourage you to lean into His saving work, rather than the work of your hands, by praying this prayer based on Romans 10:9: "Heavenly Father, I am a sinner in need of forgiveness. I confess my sins and declare with my mouth that Jesus is Lord. I believe with my heart that Jesus died on the cross for my sins and was resurrected. Amen."

Week Two

She selects wool and flax
and works with eager hands.
She is like the merchant ships,
bringing her food from afar.
She gets up while it is still night;
she provides food for her family
and portions for her female servants.

PROVERBS 31:13–15

Day 1

In this passage, we are introduced to the many strengths this woman exhibits. But what exactly does it mean to "select wool and flax"? And what's the deal with those merchant ships? In biblical times, before plastic or factories existed, wool and flax were versatile and valuable resources; fine linen, for example, was made from flax. Back then, merchant ships were the equivalent of today's shopping malls. These ships would dock at ports and bring goods, food, clothing, and other items from distant lands for all to enjoy. The Proverbs 31 woman is like these merchant ships in that she also provides things of great value: the work of her hands and her servant heart. She is wise in her choices of goods, and she delights in serving others.

Now, if you're like me, you may have started hyperventilating when you got to the part that says, "She gets up while it's still night." Maybe you felt overwhelmed and inadequate with a tinge of jealousy as you compared this woman's accomplishments to yours. But keep in mind as you read this passage that the work of our hands varies, depending on our skills, the season of life we're in, our resources, and so on. Galatians 6:4–5 warns us to pay attention to our own work and not compare ourselves to others because, at the end of the day, we are each responsible for our own conduct.

Don't let comparison steal your joy. There's no need to wish away your circumstances or complain about your lot. Focus on the work He's given you in this season and be faithful with what you have. When you surrender the work of your hands to God, He will use you for His glory right where He has you.

What are the less obvious ways in which God is calling you to serve others? Take a moment and thank God for giving you the ability and opportunity to be His hands and feet for those around you.

Day 2

When you read Proverbs 31:13–15, images of God's love might not be the first thing to come to mind. But I can't think of a better way to start day 2. Throughout this week, you'll notice a lot of doing and serving taking place, so it's important to begin our analysis at the foundation from which the motivation to serve should flow: His unconditional love.

For many years, I believed that love was earned. I knew that God loved me unconditionally, but I didn't really understand what that meant. So when I married my husband 17 years ago, I brought that belief system into our marriage.

I don't recall the details of our first argument, but I remember that I was mean and hurtful with my words. Afterward, I just assumed we were done speaking for the day, because isn't that what happens when you're mad at someone? But to my surprise, he immediately started talking to me about something in a normal, kind tone of voice. Later in the day, he even helped me with a project. I was speechless. Why was he still behaving in a loving way? He simply loved me with his actions and didn't expect anything in return? When I said "I do," I had no idea how God would use my husband to give me glimpses of His unconditional love over and over again. I still get teary-eyed thinking about it.

God's unconditional love and servant's heart are displayed on every page in the Bible. Think about what happens in the Garden of Eden after Adam and Eve sin: God goes looking for Adam and Eve in the garden because they're hiding in shame. But when He finds them, He covers their shame with a beautiful act of grace. Out of His rich mercy, He makes garments for them and clothes them (Genesis 3:21).

We can also be His hands and feet as we display His love. In Proverbs 31:13–15, we get glimpses of a woman using her influence to display God's love to those around her, right where she's at.

1. Share a time when God used someone to show you His unconditional love.

_____

_____

_____

_____

_____

_____

_____

_____

_____

_____

2. Share a time that God's love freed you to forgive another person or serve that hard-to-love person.

_____

_____

_____

_____

_____

_____

_____

_____

_____

Day 3

As you saw in verses 13 to 15, a woman of valor is depicted as someone who works hard, serves others, and provides for her family. All of these are noble qualities. There's nothing wrong with wanting to serve God and others; in fact, 1 Corinthians 15:58 says to "give yourselves fully to the work of the Lord, because you know that your labor in the Lord is not in vain."

But a problem arises if your whole identity is based on the hats you wear and the labels you carry. Having been in women's ministry for about two decades, I'm very familiar with women's desire to serve others. But sometimes, that gets in the way of spending time with God. Just like self-care is needed, so is soul care.

Let's take a look at two women of valor in the New Testament: Martha and Mary. Martha, who had a tender heart for serving others, was upset when her sister Mary sat listening to Jesus teach rather than helping her serve their guests. But Jesus responded, "Martha, Martha . . . you are worried and upset about many things, but few things are needed—or indeed only one. Mary has chosen what is better, and it will not be taken away from her" (Luke 10:41–42). Choose what is better.

In the midst of working hard and providing for and serving others, don't forget the one thing needed is time with Jesus. In Psalm 23:5, the Lord Himself invites us to feast with Him at the table He's prepared for us. You, my sister, are invited to the table—not to serve or help clean up, but to enjoy His presence.

1. How often do you ignore the invitation to spend time with God because you're too busy serving Him or others?

_____

_____

_____

_____

_____

_____

_____

_____

_____

2. What do you need to remove or change in order for you to make time to be in God's Word?

_____

_____

_____

_____

_____

_____

_____

_____

_____

Day 4

When we are in Christ, God can't stop loving us! The real us. The rebellious us. The unfaithful us. But, believing that can be so hard. Why? Well, for starters, there are simply too many parts of us that feel so unlovable.

—JEANNIE CUNNION

As we ponder this week's passage and the work that goes into choosing wool, waking up when it's still dark out, and joyfully serving, let's pause to reflect on the motivation behind our service: His never-ending love.

You are marked by God's love, not by your mistakes. Love that's based on your performance can never replace His unconditional love.

Guided Prayer

Heavenly Father, let me live convinced that nothing can ever separate me from Your love, neither death nor life, neither angels nor demons, neither fears for today nor my worries for tomorrow (Romans 8:38). Neither my good works nor lack thereof can make You love me more or less. Open my eyes to see how You can use the work of my hands for Your glory. In Jesus's name, amen.

Day 5

The Lord recently directed me through a season I have named "release and receive." What does that mean? Well, at a very young age, I learned a simple formula: hard work + service + intellect = love! As a mom, wife, counselor, community leader, and missionary, this formula served me well. I was applauded, recognized, given awards, and loved by many. I believed that the more I served, the more I would be loved. Yes, the world rewarded my service ... but God was not so impressed with my motives.

We serve God because *we are* loved, not *in order to be* loved. I confused my accomplishments with my identity, and it left me exhausted and frustrated. I was endlessly trying to prove that His redeeming work on the cross was not wasted on me. Deep down inside, I feared that if I wasn't earning my keep, then I wasn't worthy of His love. We are not given the details of how the Proverbs 31 woman feels about her situation, but I bet that, like so many women, she's been tempted to confuse what she does with who she is.

This is where my "release and receive" comes in. I had to *release* my grip on the idea that my hard work made me worthy so my heart could be awakened to *receive* God's love and grace just as I am. Needless to say, the process was excruciating. I truly enjoyed helping others and teaching God's Word through my work and service! But somewhere along the way, these gifts began robbing my heart of rest. He led me through a time of removing all the hats I wore and labels I tirelessly carried. I fought God over and over again as He chiseled away at yet another label I wore to prove I was worthy of His love. For six months, God whispered this truth to me in various ways:

"Come to Me, and I will give you rest. I love you, brokenness and all. I love you in your mess. I love you with an everlasting love."

The paradox of it all is my life had to unravel in order for me to become whole again. Once I came face-to-face with my brokenness and inability to "fix" the world around me, the healing began. I gave myself permission to cry, be weak, receive help from others, and receive comfort from God—to accept His love not for what I brought to the table but simply because I am a daughter of the King. Sometimes in order for your faith to grow, you need to fall apart. In that brokenness, you'll find freedom. The freedom to live loved!

Have you ever felt like love and acceptance is based on what you bring to the table? If so, what caused you to feel that way?

_____

_____

_____

_____

_____

_____

_____

_____

_____

_____

Day 6

You might think that . . . your giftedness or your personality type or your job title . . . somehow defines you. But in reality, it is your desire for God and your capacity to reach for more of God than you have right now.

—RUTH HALEY BARTON

Using your gifts but not letting them define you is a tension we learn to balance throughout our lives. In this week's Proverbs 31 passage, we learn how one woman uses her abilities to provide for those among whom God has given her influence. So let's discover your strengths!

Below is a list of character traits found in Proverbs 31. Circle your top three strengths from the list.

Dependable	**Fearless**
Flexible	**Faithful**
Resilient	**Visionary**
Creative	**Thoughtful**
Organized	**Generous**
Bold	**Frugal**
Hardworking	**Wise**
Caring	**Compassionate**
Just	

Now write one way that God has helped you use each strength in the sphere of influence He has given you.

Strength #1: _____

_____

_____

_____

_____

Strength #2: _____

_____

_____

_____

_____

_____

_____

Strength #3: _____

_____

_____

_____

_____

_____

_____

Day 7

You've completed week two—almost. Let's slow down and spend some extra time in the Word today, reviewing what we've discussed over the past week and thinking about how we'll put it into action in our lives.

Review

Here's what we talked about this week.

→ In the midst of working hard, providing, and serving others, don't forget to choose what is better: time at the feet of Jesus.
→ Service is a beautiful response to His love, but we serve Him because *we* love *Him*, not because we are striving to earn His love. Live loved.
→ His love is what motivates us to serve, and that love also guides us to set boundaries.
→ Don't let the fruit of His gifts go to waste by comparing yourself to others, wishing away your circumstances, or complaining about your lot.
→ Harness the work of your hands and be faithful with what he has given you.

Discuss

Answer these questions on your own or in a group.

1. What did you learn this week that brought you comfort?

_____

_____

_____

_____

_____

_____

_____

_____

_____

_____

2. Matthew 20:28 says Jesus "did not come to be served, but
   to serve, and to give his life as a ransom for many." How does
   knowing that Jesus was a beautiful example of a servant
   leader motivate you in your service?

_____

_____

_____

_____

_____

_____

_____

_____

_____

_____

3. What connections do you see between His love and our service?

_____

_____

_____

_____

_____

_____

_____

_____

_____

4. What are some obstacles you face when serving others?

_____

_____

_____

_____

_____

_____

_____

_____

_____

_____

5. Share how you're going to use your specific strengths in your sphere of influence.

_____

_____

_____

_____

_____

_____

_____

Act

Here are some things you can do in the next week to put the lessons you've learned into action.

→ Memorize Ephesians 2:10: "For we are God's handiwork, created in Christ Jesus to do good works, which God prepared in advance for us to do."

→ Ask God to help you understand His love in a deeper way.

→ Make a plan for spending more time in God's Word. Be specific about when you'll do it, how often, and what you'll study. Keep it simple, especially if this is new to you. Then ask a friend to help keep you accountable.

→ Think of an act of kindness you can perform this week, and do it!

Week Three

She considers a field and buys it;
out of her earnings she plants a vineyard.
She sets about her work vigorously;
her arms are strong for her tasks.
She sees that her trading is profitable,
and her lamp does not go out at night.
In her hand she holds the distaff
and grasps the spindle with her fingers.

PROVERBS 31:16–19

Day 1

When my boys were little, they loved doing exercise videos with me. I'd watch as they flailed their uncoordinated arms around with determination on their faces. After a few seconds of "exercising," they'd run over to show me their muscles, exclaiming, "Mommy, I'm strong!" I chuckle at the memory—but then I realize how often I mimic their words, hoping "my arms will be strong for my tasks" without having to work for it. So often we want quick relief and fast deliverance. It takes time to plant a vineyard, develop strong arms, and build a profitable business; these things did not happen overnight for the Proverbs 31 woman. Yet we want an order of immediate results, please!

But character is built over a lifetime, and that's what you see painted in this week's verses: a lifetime of virtues developed. Proverbs 31 is made up of snapshots in the different seasons of the life of a woman who lives out wisdom among her family and community.

I've never planted a vineyard like she does in verse 16, but I've watched my Amish neighbors work their fields, and I understand it takes months of preparation and hard work before a seed even goes down. We like to go to God asking for a ripe, juicy helping of faithfulness, courage, and love, but instead, He hands us seeds. We often forget that He is in all of it. He's in the tilling of the soil, the planting of the seeds, and the life-giving rain. In Philippians 2:12–13, we are told that, though our salvation is a gift, the work of our hands is evidence of our faith. So in prayer and with hope, you work and trust Him for the fruit of your vineyard—faithfulness, courage, love, diligence, wisdom, determination—to spring forth.

Those of us who don't do much farming or gardening often forget there are seasons and stages in the cultivation process. We think of that "waiting" season as a passive state where nothing is happening.

But really it's the exact opposite. This middle ground is fertile soil, perfect to grow a powerful prayer life as you allow the Lord to work within you. It's tempting to want to rush past it or ask God to take it away. But what if God wants you to stay and open your eyes to see His goodness, love, and grace unfold in the waiting?

As women, we have many seasons of life, and in the hands of God nothing is wasted. Perhaps you find yourself in a season of potty-training toddlers, changing careers, empty-nesting, looking for your special someone, or grieving a loss. Regardless of where you are, remember the Lord's goodness can be found in the waiting, the chaos, the changes, and the loss.

1. What is your response to a season in life when God has you waiting?

_____

_____

_____

_____

_____

_____

_____

_____

_____

_____

2. After reading today's encouragement, what do you think God would have you do?

_____

_____

_____

_____

_____

_____

_____

_____

_____

Day 2

Reflect for a moment on the events after Jesus was crucified on Good Friday. In Luke 24:13–32, we see how this time between the cross and His resurrection was a hard season of waiting for the disciples. But then, to their surprise, Jesus met two of them on the road to Emmaus in the midst of their distress. Now consider a time when you found yourself in a waiting season. Write down some of the challenges that took place, and then write down how God met you in the mess.

_____

_____

_____

_____

_____

_____

_____

_____

_____

_____

_____

When I read this week's verses, I see a woman with wisdom, strength, diligence, resilience, determination, and moxie. What character traits have you seen God build in you as a result of the challenging seasons you just wrote about? How did those challenges build those strengths?

_____

_____

_____

_____

_____

_____

_____

_____

_____

_____

Day 3

Most of us consider waiting to be wasting.
But it's not so with our God. God works
while we wait.

—LOUIE GIGLIO

Guided Prayer

Heavenly Father, the waiting period, the interlude, the messy middle, is so utterly hard. But You, Lord, You waste nothing. Open my eyes to see Your goodness at work in my life right now where You have me. Teach me to surrender the messy middle and rest in Your truth that the good work You began You will finish to the end. In Your name, amen.

Day 4

This week's passage says that our Proverbs 31 woman "sets about her work vigorously; her arms are strong for her tasks." Where does a woman of valor find that kind of strength?

As a child, I sat in the back of our maroon van on the way home from church every Wednesday night, listening to the local Christian radio station's program spotlighting different heroes of faith. These were my "but God" stories—stories of missionaries who didn't try to write a period where God has placed a comma. Each hardship they encountered was followed by the two most redeeming words mankind could ever hear: "But God . . ." We see it in Genesis 50:20, in the life of Joseph: "You intended to harm me, but God intended it for good to accomplish what is now being done." The enemy never triumphs; God's light always overcomes the darkness.

Many years later, I was given a cassette tape that told the story of a missionary named Darlene D. Rose, a woman of valor—faithful, hardworking, compassionate, and resilient. It turned out to be a recording of the program I'd listened to as a child. I was struck by Darlene's life story, which involved, among other things, intense suffering in a Japanese POW camp during World War II. As Dr. Daniel Akin wrote in an article on the International Mission Board's website:

> The brutal conditions of a WWII Japanese internment camp included near-starvation, forced labor, inhumane conditions, false accusations of espionage, serious illnesses, solitary confinement, and torture. Through it all, Darlene was sustained by God, who never left her nor forsook her, just as he promised. He remained her light and salvation.

Darlene's strength in the Lord was evident through her prayer life. The cassette recounted how Darlene and her husband were missionaries in Papua New Guinea when World War II broke out and the Japanese military invaded the country. Early on in the invasion, she was hiding out in her home, praying fervently for God's protection, when thieves broke in—but they didn't take anything. After that night, the thieves waited outside her home for the right moment to attack again, but they never did. Much later, after the war was over, she saw one of them. She asked him, "Why did you all just stand outside my home?" His response was one of her many "but God" moments. He said, "We were afraid of those big men dressed in white that surrounded your home." Nothing goes unseen on His watch. He holds the beginning, the messy middle, and the end of our story.

You may not be able to relate to Darlene's exact circumstances, but you've certainly gone through your own seasons of fear, loneliness, or sadness. Ponder for a moment one of your "but God" stories that highlights how God never leaves you (for example, "I was driving home with my toddler when a car hit us, *but God* protected us and no one was hurt"). Write it down below and share His goodness with someone this week.

_____

_____

_____

_____

_____

Day 5

Here's a more familiar "but God" story: Hagar's. In the book of Genesis, Sarah, unable to conceive a child of her own, gives her slave girl, Hagar, to her husband, Abraham, in hopes of producing the child whom God had promised them through her. But when Hagar becomes pregnant, Sarah mistreats her. Hagar flees into the desert, where, without food or water, she is sure to die.

Here's where her "but God" moment happens. Our all-knowing, gracious God sends an angel of the Lord to find her. He doesn't call her a slave girl. He calls her by name. He comforts her and reminds her of who God is and whom she belongs to. In that moment, she gives God a name: *El Roi*, "the God who sees me" (Genesis 16:13). God didn't just see Hagar's circumstances. He saw her heart, her pain, her worries, and her feelings.

Though Hagar's circumstances were different from those of the Proverbs 31 woman, we can see so many of the godly virtues of a woman of valor evident in her life. In the midst of mistreatment and abuse, Hagar displays courage, determination, and fear of the Lord. We also see obedience: God asks her to go back to Abraham and Sarah, and she does.

Scripture doesn't give us all the details of her emotional state, but I think it's safe to say Hagar felt lonely, sad, and used, like all her hard work and service had been taken for granted by Sarah and Abraham. After all, she was carrying their baby, but they still abused her! Maybe she even felt like God had forgotten her. But He had not.

At some point in your life you may have felt forgotten, overlooked, or unappreciated in the midst of serving God and others. When was the last time you felt unseen or misunderstood? Why? Instead of shoving those feelings down, bring them to God and let Him minister to your heart. Ask Him to comfort you and guide you. We need to remember in the darkness what God has told us in the light. He will help you recall to whom you belong and who He is. He is the God who sees and the God who looks after you.

Write down a list of the five things you do or have done that don't/didn't receive any acknowledgment or gratitude. Write it out like this: "You are the God who sees _____. Help me _____." For example, "You are the God who sees me cleaning up around the house and making it a restful place. Help me resist feeling resentful when my children constantly make a mess."

1. _____
   _____

2. _____
   _____

3. _____
   _____

4. _____
   _____

5. _____
   _____

Day 6

Proverbs 31 is a celebration of women! In fact, there's a Jewish custom for men to honor the women in their life at the Shabbat meal by reciting or singing Proverbs 31: 10–31 to them. This week, looking at Proverbs 31: 16–19, we've celebrated wisdom, good stewardship, strength, diligence, resilience, and more.

Who is one of your "heroes of faith," a woman you may not know personally but who has set an example for you? Write her name on the line provided. (If you don't have one, I highly recommend you read about Darlene D. Rose, Corrie ten Boom, or Rosa Parks.)

_____

Now reflect on the women of valor in your life who display the qualities featured in this week's Proverbs 31 verses. Write down the names of three women and the ways you can lean into their godly character and learn from them. For example, you could message one of them and say, "Hey, I noticed you're really good at stewarding your finances. I'd love to hear any tips you'd be willing to share with me that have helped you."

1. _____

_____

2. _____

_____

3. _____

_____

Day 7

You've reached the end of another week of Bible study! Celebrate by spending some extra time reviewing, discussing, and deciding how to act, either on your own or with your small group.

Review

Here's what we talked about this week.

→ We often desire fast results at the cost of the lessons we can learn and the character we can develop through hardship. But the Lord's goodness can be found in the waiting, the chaos, the changes, and the loss. God is at work; nothing is wasted.

→ Don't place a period where God has placed a comma.

→ God is intimately aware of your fears, loneliness, sadness, and suffering. He sees you.

→ Because He is the God who sees, you can surrender the work of your hands to Him.

Discuss

Answer these questions on your own or in a group.

1. Why do you think it's so hard to see God in the midst of the waiting?

_____

_____

_____

_____

_____

_____

_____

_____

_____

2. What surprised you most during this week's lessons?

_____

_____

_____

_____

_____

_____

_____

_____

_____

_____

_____

3. How will knowing that God is *El Roi* and is intimately
   acquainted with you bring you comfort this week as you serve
   Him and others?

_____

_____

_____

_____

_____

_____

_____

_____

_____

4. What challenged you most from this week's study?

_____

_____

_____

_____

_____

_____

_____

_____

_____

_____

Act

Here are some things you can do in the next week to put the lessons you've learned into action.

→ Read Psalm 139:1–5.
→ Think of one person who needs to be reminded that God is _El Roi_ and tell them how much you value their work. Or maybe they need to hear that God knows them by name, sees them, and cares for them.
→ When you notice a "but God" moment happening, write it down in a notebook. At the end of the week, see how many you've experienced.

Week Four

She opens her arms to the poor
and extends her hands to the needy.
When it snows, she has no fear for her household;
for all of them are clothed in scarlet.
She makes coverings for her bed;
she is clothed in fine linen and purple.

PROVERBS 31:20–22

Day 1

After observing a godly woman in action, have you ever asked yourself, "How does she do it?" This is the question that runs through many of our minds as we read this week's passage in Proverbs 31. How is the woman of valor so generous, opening her arms to the poor and extending her hands to the needy? Why is she not afraid of the severe consequences to her family's health and livelihood that might be caused by snow?

Our lives are forever changed when we fully know and remember that God is *Jehovah Jireh*, a title that comes from a Hebrew phrase meaning "the Lord will provide." It is first mentioned in Genesis 22, when Abraham is asked to sacrifice his own son, Isaac. By faith, Abraham brings Isaac to the altar, knowing that God will provide another sacrifice—and He does. A ram appears and takes Isaac's place, and thus Abraham named that place "the Lord will provide."

Our God will provide, just as He provided a sacrifice for Abraham, an ark for Noah, manna for the Israelites, and Jesus Christ as the ultimate sacrifice for our sins. Sometimes it's easy to doubt His provision and His plan for our lives, so we take matters into our own hands. Many times His provision looks different from what we anticipated. But God has never left us out to die. He always provides for His children.

The way we live our lives as a result of knowing Him intimately spills over to those around us. That is why we can "open our hands to the poor and extend our hands to the needy."

Behind every generous woman's heart is a woman who clings to her *Jehovah Jireh*. Will you open your eyes to see that His provisions and gifts have one purpose—to lead us to the Giver?

Day 2

Turn to page 71 and reread this week's Proverbs 31 passage, looking for the character traits of a godly woman. Then answer the questions below.

1. What godly virtue do you see in verse 20? How about in verses 21 and 22?

_____

_____

_____

_____

_____

_____

_____

_____

_____

_____

2. Which one of these would you say is your strongest character trait? Why? Thank God for your strengths.

_____

_____

_____

_____

_____

_____

_____

_____

_____

3. Which one of these would you say is your weakest character trait? Why? Offer your weaknesses up to God.

_____

_____

_____

_____

_____

_____

_____

_____

_____

Day 3

We are made in His image and crafted as a vessel to contain His spirit. He longs to fill us with more of himself but we have to be willing.

—ELISA PULLIAM

Throughout all of scripture, we see God as our provider. He provides us with comfort, the Holy Spirit, grace, power, love, salvation, and peace. In John 14:27, Jesus says, "Peace I leave with you; my peace I give you. I do not give to you as the world does. Do not let your hearts be troubled and do not be afraid." The Proverbs 31 woman has no fear for her household because her faith is deeply rooted in the knowledge that God can be trusted.

But you see, the kind of trust in God this woman exhibits doesn't just happen; it's developed in close proximity to our Savior. It's a trust that believes He will provide in the face of uncertainty and confusion. As we spend time in His Word, we allow the Holy Spirit to gently pry our hands open to our Provider. We allow the Spirit of God to whisper His truth to our forgetful hearts, reminding us that He is not withholding anything good from us (Psalm 84:11). From that openness in our hearts and spirits, a heart of compassion and generosity overflows.

Guided Prayer

Heavenly Father, we look to You! We reach toward You with open hearts because You are *Jehovah Jireh,* the Lord who provides for us yesterday, today, and forevermore. Forgive us, for You know we struggle with spiritual amnesia. Teach our hearts to remember that You can be trusted and Your provisions deeply satisfy us. Open our eyes to see Your goodness and blessings. May we respond in gratitude for the various ways You provide for us. In Your name, amen.

Day 4

Here's a story about a time when spiritual amnesia (forgetting that God's love can be trusted) got to me. My family and I were missionaries in Ecuador for nine years. When we left the mission field, we were led to give away most of our belongings, in faith, knowing that all we owned was God's and He would provide for our future. At first, I felt like the Proverbs 31 woman, opening my hands to others, unafraid of snow for my household. I wasn't scared!

That is, until things began to unravel. One problem after another plagued us, but it was our car situation that broke me. We spent several months putting the sale of our car in order. Because we trusted the buyers, we transferred the car's title to them without receiving payment. Then we received a text saying they were backing out and no longer wanted the car, even though they now legally owned it!

We felt betrayed, heartbroken, and confused. We left the mission field—and our community of dear friends—with an unsold car, no home, and no jobs. This week's verses describe making fine linen clothes and sheets, but we didn't even have beds, much less coverings for them. All we had was a few suitcases and a lot of confusion. I cried many nights, wondering if God had forgotten us. Was He for us? Would He really provide? Like the Israelites wandering the desert in the book of Exodus, I questioned why God brought us this far only to leave us out to die.

But that was far from the truth. Yes, our situation was difficult, but there wasn't a day that God didn't send manna down from heaven for us. Friends and family back in the United States showered us with all of the belongings we'd just given away in Ecuador—everything from pots and pans to, yes, bedsheets. After living in temporary housing for over a year, my prayer for us to be in a permanent home before our boys started school was answered.

And if that wasn't enough, the original car buyer who broke our trust apologized. We also sold the car we'd left in Ecuador. God's provisions didn't always follow our "perfect" plan, but nevertheless God provided.

You may be in a season when God can use you to provide for others. Or maybe you find yourself in a time where you're unable to provide for your family's physical, emotional, or spiritual needs—but don't underestimate God's power. Wherever you may find yourself in this stage of life, be assured that *Jehovah Jireh* will provide. He can be trusted with every detail of your life. You're not powerful enough to mess up God's plan—no one is. Our God is forever faithful. No problem is too big for Him, no enemy too fierce, no sin too evil for Him to handle. He's in the job of redeeming our circumstances, hurt, and sin.

1. How do you respond to Jesus in the midst of a season of unraveling?

_____

_____

_____

_____

_____

_____

_____

_____

_____

_____

2. What brings you back to trusting in His promises?

_____

_____

_____

_____

_____

_____

_____

_____

Day 5

He has chosen not to heal me, but to hold me.

—JONI EARECKSON TADA

What does "she is clothed in fine linen and purple" mean, exactly? Let's look at this line in Proverbs 31:22: the woman of valor takes pride in her outer appearance with her fine garments. As Michael Krauszer points out, in scripture, "fine linen and purple" often represent honor, worth, and righteousness, so the poem is celebrating her beyond just what she's wearing. She's clothed in good deeds and noble acts as she reflects Christ's righteousness.

Joni Eareckson Tada—author, radio host, and disability advocate—is a beautiful example of a woman of valor who clothes herself in Christ's righteousness. Although she was paralyzed from the shoulders down in a diving accident, she has faithfully trusted *Jehovah Jireh*. Because she knows the Lord has provided and will provide, she overflows with God's comfort for others. She has open hands to serve and an open heart to accept God's provision for her life. She leans into what God has done for her so she can reflect His righteousness.

1. In what way can you clothe yourself with Christ's righteousness as you serve others?

_____

_____

_____

_____

_____

_____

_____

_____

_____

2. Can you describe an instance in which you were challenged to believe God would show himself faithful? In what way can you allow God to provide for you?

_____

_____

_____

_____

_____

_____

_____

_____

_____

Day 6

Look over the following list and rate how often you believe each lie on a scale from 1 to 5, with 1 being "rarely or never" and 5 being "on a regular basis." The enemy loves to confuse you, so take a second to bask in God's love and presence as you read each truth.

Lie #1: God doesn't care about me.

1   2   3   4   5

Truth: "Consider the ravens: They do not sow or reap, they have no storeroom or barn; yet God feeds them. And how much more valuable you are than birds!" (Luke 12:24)

Lie #2: God is holding out on me.

1   2   3   4   5

Truth: "If you, then, though you are evil, know how to give good gifts to your children, how much more will your Father in heaven give good gifts to those who ask him!" (Matthew 7:11)

Lie #3: God has forgotten about me.

1   2   3   4   5

Truth: "Can a mother forget the baby at her breast and have no compassion on the child she has borne? Though she may forget, I will not forget you!" (Isaiah 49:15)

Day 7

Congratulations, you made it to the end of week 4! Let's go beyond five minutes today as we review and discuss the past week and think about what actions we'll take in the next.

Review

Here's what we talked about this week.

→ Inside every generous woman is a heart that clings to her *Jehovah Jireh.*

→ Neither you nor anyone else is powerful enough to mess up God's plan.

→ God does not abandon His people.

→ God always provides for His children, although often not in the way we envisioned. Wherever you may find yourself in this season, be assured that *Jehovah Jireh* will provide.

Discuss

Answer these questions on your own or in a group.

1. Where do you sense God calling you to take action as you extend your hands to the needy?

_____

_____

_____

_____

_____

_____

_____

_____

2. What is weighing heavy on your heart today as you think about your own fears for the future? Take it to God and remind yourself that He will provide.

_____

_____

_____

_____

_____

_____

_____

_____

_____

_____

3. When have you seen God turn something challenging in your life into a blessing?

_____

_____

_____

_____

_____

_____

_____

_____

_____

Act

Here are some things you can do in the next week to put the lessons you've learned into action.

→ Identify one thing you need to mute in order to hear how God would have you serve within the sphere of influence in which He has placed you.

→ In Philippians 4:12, the apostle Paul writes, "I know what it is to be in need, and I know what it is to have plenty. I have learned the secret of being content in any and every situation, whether well fed or hungry, whether living in plenty or in want." Start praying this verse in the morning before you get out of bed to remind yourself that you have nothing to fear.

→ Every night when you lie down to sleep, thank God for three things from your day.

Week Five

Her husband is respected at the city gate,
where he takes his seat among the elders
   of the land.
She makes linen garments and sells them,
and supplies the merchants with sashes.
She is clothed with strength and dignity;
she can laugh at the days to come.

PROVERBS 31:23–25

Day 1

I hope by now I've convinced you that Proverbs 31 is not a checklist you can never measure up to but rather an image of what we look like when we live out our identity in Christ. It's the work of Jesus Christ in our hearts that people see as He daily refines and molds us to be more like Him.

Maybe you rushed past the verse about sewing and selling in this week's passage because you've never considered yourself the creative type or entrepreneurial endeavors aren't really your cup of tea. Well, it's a good thing we're looking at the character traits exhibited in each verse rather than the specific actions. What we see in this passage is a woman who has the initiative to take what God has blessed her with (for example, sewing and business skills) and use it for His glory. Whatever God has called you to, He will equip you for it. God has equipped us with every spiritual blessing for the season of life He has us in, "for we are God's handiwork, created in Christ Jesus to do good works, which God prepared in advance for us to do" (Ephesians 2:10).

Now, we don't know much about this woman of valor's personality. She could be an introvert or a social butterfly, serious or hilarious. But we do know that her life brings honor to her husband, her family, and her whole community because "her husband is respected at the city gate, where he takes his seat among the elders." (It would have been difficult to achieve that position if his spouse was being a negative influence on the people around them.) You don't have to be onstage or lead loudly in order to lead with strength and dignity. Women of valor come in all personality types and demeanors. The way we live our lives always leads people either closer to God or further away from Him.

What is one way God can use *your* wiring and personality to influence the people around you this week?

_____

_____

_____

_____

_____

_____

_____

_____

_____

Day 2

Are you trying to be who Jesus wants you to be? Or do you trust him to bring out who he has already created you to be?

—EMILY FREEMAN

Is there a woman in your life who can use some encouragement as she discovers her influence for God's glory? Today, pray for her to understand she can have an impact right where God has placed her. Then write her a note letting her know you're praying for wherever God has her or whatever He is moving her toward.

Guided Prayer

Heavenly Father, we praise You for Your faithfulness toward us and for never giving up on the good work You began in our lives. As women, our seasons of life are constantly changing, whether it's physically or circumstantially, but You are never-changing. May our confidence and hope always be anchored in Your unfailing love and not our gifts, abilities, or skills. May we remember the grass withers and the flowers fade, but Your word lasts forever (Isaiah 40:8). Amen.

Day 3

So put on Christ. Clothe yourselves with Christ. . . . Never be without the covering of Christ. Let your friendship with Christ be as close as the shirt you wear.

—JOHN PIPER

The Proverbs 31 woman is "clothed with" godly virtues in verse 25. Let's take a look at a few examples of what scripture says we can clothe ourselves with.

→ "For all of you who were baptized into Christ have clothed yourselves with Christ." (Galatians 3:27)
→ "Rather, clothe yourselves with the Lord Jesus Christ, and do not think about how to gratify the desires of the flesh." (Romans 13:14)
→ "Therefore, as God's chosen people, holy and dearly loved, clothe yourselves with compassion, kindness, humility, gentleness and patience.... And over all these virtues put on love, which binds them together in perfect unity." (Colossians 3:12, 14)

In Colossians 3:8, before instructing the church to put on compassion and love, Paul tells them to first "rid yourselves of" evil desires, rage, malice, gossip, and slander, among other things. In other words, you can't put on clean clothes until you've taken off the dirt-stained clothes you're wearing. Part of clothing yourself with Christ is removing those evil desires.

This is God's message to us in Proverbs 31. As daughters of the King, we can put on compassion and love. Whatever season of life we're in, we can be clothed with Christ.

It takes a woman of valor filled with God's power to put off evil desires and put on strength and dignity. With what do you seek to clothe yourself?

Day 4

What does Proverbs 31:25 mean when it says a woman of valor "can laugh at the days to come"?

In our culture today, a woman of strong character is sometimes seen as controlling, disrespectful, or arrogant. But a godly woman of strength is anything but those things. Proverbs 31 shows us that a woman of strength fears the Lord, knows her God, and lives in accordance with His truth. What is the fruit we see in someone who knows and abides in Him? It's woven into each verse of this passage: love. The woman of valor's love for God is demonstrated in her actions toward her family and community. True strength of character is displayed in a woman who is confident in God—not in her circumstances, role, or gifts. She is strong, courageous, fearless, and not discouraged because the Lord her God is with her wherever she goes (Joshua 1:9).

Have you ever seen the movie *The Chronicles of Narnia: Prince Caspian*, based on the C. S. Lewis book? Prince Caspian is at war with his uncle. At one point, it seems like the bad guys will win. King Peter is outnumbered, and the enemy comes rushing toward them. But then you see little Lucy, a young woman of valor, bold and fierce in the face of danger. She stands at the front line of this battle with great courage, holding only a dagger. There are hundreds of enemy soldiers ready to come at her, but she's fearless. And then you see *why* she's able to stand before the army: The great lion Aslan joins her and defeats their enemies.

That is what I envision when I read the verse "She can laugh at the days to come." We can be fearless about what lies ahead because we know that, like Aslan with Lucy, the Lord goes before us, stands beside us, and is in us.

Day 5

Worry and fear can keep you from living with confidence and trust in God. Today let's focus on some ways you can rest in God's faithfulness and "laugh at the days to come."

1. What kinds of things in your life commonly trigger worry or fear?

_____

_____

_____

_____

_____

_____

_____

_____

_____

_____

2. The next time one of the things you mentioned above comes up, how can you turn that worry into worship? (One rec-ommendation: Read Psalm 16 and ask God to help you take refuge in Him.)

_____

_____

_____

_____

_____

_____

_____

_____

_____

_____

_____

3. One of the Hebrew names for God is *El Emunah*, which means "the faithful God" (Deuteronomy 32:4). How can you rest in God's faithfulness today instead of trying to muster up strength and courage on your own?

_____

_____

_____

_____

_____

_____

_____

_____

_____

Day 6

When I think of a biblical woman of valor who has the initiative to take what God has blessed her with and use it for His glory, Queen Esther comes to mind. When given the opportunity to either save her people or stay quiet, Esther faces her fear head-on as a woman clothed in strength and dignity. She exhibits determination and courage in God's sovereignty in the face of danger.

Esther is fearless and "laughs at the future" because she knows her God parted the sea for Moses, provided for Abraham, and made the wall fall down for Joshua, and He is the same God who is with her. The words of her forefathers ring in her heart: "Know therefore that the Lord your God is God; he is the faithful God, keeping his covenant of love to a thousand generations of those who love him and keep his commandments" (Deuteronomy 7:9).

One of the most powerful lines in the book of Esther is found in 4:16, where she says, "If I perish, I perish." She runs the risk of dying, yet she confidently stands her ground and boldly moves forward, trusting God's bigger plan and purpose. She laughs at the days to come because she expects God to be what He says He is: faithful!

1. Think about what Esther's story tells us. What's one step you can take this week to better live in light of this truth?

_____

_____

_____

_____

_____

_____

_____

_____

_____

_____

2. Now write down one thing you would like to see God help you accomplish this year, and ask Him to show you how this one thing can be used for His glory.

_____

_____

_____

_____

_____

_____

_____

_____

_____

Day 7

Now that we've reached the end of another week of five-minute lessons, let's spend a little longer with God's Word today.

Review

Here's what we discussed this week.

→ Proverbs 31 tells us about character traits rather than specific actions. We each have different gifts and abilities we can use for God's glory.

→ You must "take off" your old self in order to clothe yourself with Christ.

→ We can be fearless about the future and confident in who we are because we know God is with us. He is what He says He is: faithful!

→ The same God who parted the sea for Moses, provided for Abraham, knocked down the wall for Joshua, and made Esther fearless is with you.

Discuss

Answer these questions on your own or in a group.

1. Read Proverbs 31:23. How does the way we behave reflect the way we perceive God?

_____

_____

_____

_____

_____

_____

_____

_____

2. What can you be grateful for today and praise Him about?

_____

_____

_____

_____

_____

_____

_____

_____

_____

_____

3. Does knowing that God is faithful bring you peace? Why or why not?

_____

_____

_____

_____

_____

_____

_____

_____

_____

4. Think of a moment in your life when you were unafraid of the future. Where were you? What were you doing? What can you learn from that moment?

_____

_____

_____

_____

_____

_____

_____

_____

_____

_____

5. What's one truth you learned or "lightbulb moment" you had this week?

_____

_____

_____

_____

_____

_____

_____

_____

Act

Here are some things you can do in the next week to put the lessons you've learned into action.

→ Write a prayer asking God to show you His track record of faithfulness in the Bible and your life. Keep your eyes and ears open to see His faithfulness in the coming week.

→ Name two labels you have given yourself (or others have given you) that you need to let go of in order to see yourself as who God has created you to be.

→ Write down how you see God using you this year in the sphere of influence in which He has placed you. It doesn't have to involve selling linen garments you've sewn!

Week Six

She speaks with wisdom,
and faithful instruction is on her tongue.
She watches over the affairs of her household
and does not eat the bread of idleness.
Her children arise and call her blessed;
her husband also, and he praises her:
"Many women do noble things,
but you surpass them all."

PROVERBS 31:26–29

Day 1

In the Old Testament, the Hebrew word for "wisdom" is *hakhmah*, and it's an attribute of God. Wisdom is not simply intellectual knowledge; it's interwoven into every aspect of your life. Throughout scripture, a connection is repeatedly made between wisdom and God. It's not something we have of our own doing. God is the giver of wisdom because He is infinitely all-knowing.

The book of Proverbs is an example of what is known as "wisdom literature"—the books of the Bible that offer advice and aphorisms. It's attributed to King Solomon, who was sought out by people from all over the world for the wisdom God put in his heart (2 Chronicles 9:23).

James 3:17 says, "The wisdom that comes from heaven is first of all pure; then peace-loving, considerate, submissive, full of mercy and good fruit, impartial and sincere." True wisdom challenges us and calls us to live out what we claim to love and believe by speaking with knowledge and kindness, like the Proverbs 31 woman.

When life squeezes you, what is going to come out? Is it kindness that's on your tongue? When others are slandering someone, do you find yourself joining in the gossip? With social media at our finger-tips, it's gotten easier than ever to be downright mean. I don't know about you, but my mouth is not always overflowing with wisdom and faithful instruction.

In James 1:5, we are told that if we lack wisdom, we should ask for it from God, who will give it to us. It's not just learning God's wisdom but allowing that wisdom to change the way we live and the way we speak and treat others. But no one can do this by their own strength because we are sinners in need of a Savior. So we must lean into the Holy Spirit for the strength to do the next right thing.

How can you show wisdom and kindness in your thoughts and speech? Who do you know who does this well, and how can you follow that person's example?

_____

_____

_____

_____

_____

Day 2

When we stop gazing at our own inadequacies,
we are free to celebrate that God uses us
despite them.

—SUZANNE ELLER

It took a little growing up for me to realize that not every mother overflows with wisdom and purpose like mine. As a child I took it for granted (and as a teen I was greatly annoyed by it). But now I praise my mom for it. My mom did not let her lack of formal education keep her from being used by God. My parents were raised in a small rural village in Mexico, so neither of them received much schooling, but they brim with wisdom and have a heart to serve others. Whenever you talk to my mom, you find yourself gleaning some random nugget of wisdom that's just what you needed to hear. God uses us in spite of us! What a relief!

Guided Prayer

Lord, I praise You for the mother (or mother figures) You've given me. My life has been deeply impacted by her life. Thank You for this beautiful example of Your selflessness and compassion toward us. Teach me to be more like You. I know the more time I spend soaking in Your word and presence, the more I will overflow with Your truth and compassion. In Your name, amen.

Day 3

Proverbs 31:27 reminds us to be good stewards of our time. It says the woman of valor "watches over her household." What you watch over is what you focus on; it's what you fill your time and attention with.

1. What are some of the "affairs in your household" or life that God has entrusted you with?

_____

_____

_____

_____

_____

_____

_____

_____

_____

_____

2. Of course, the enemy loves when we "eat the bread of idleness" and only give partial attention to our first love. The enemy is cunning, disguising distractions in busyness, social media, news updates, fear, text messages, and noise. Reflect for a moment on some of your daily distractions. Remember, it can even be good things like an informative podcast or an insightful book that lure us away from what is most important. Ask God to help you be honest and write down two or three things that encourage idleness in your life.

_____

_____

_____

_____

_____

_____

_____

_____

_____

3. Now think of something life-giving with which you can replace each distraction you wrote down. For example, if you wrote, "Checking my email first thing when I wake up," you might replace it with "Reading my Bible and praying first thing when I wake up."

_____

_____

_____

_____

_____

_____

_____

_____

Day 4

Whether it's housework, childcare, going to work, or anything else, "watching over your household" can sometimes feel menial, difficult, or boring. Think about the menial tasks you perform in your day. Write down three of them, and then write a note of gratitude for each one. For example, if one of your tasks is "I have dishes to wash," the note of gratitude might be "I am thankful for the food You give us to eat."

1. Task

_____

_____

Note of gratitude

_____

_____

2. Task

_____

_____

Note of gratitude

_____

_____

3. Task

_____

_____

Note of gratitude

_____

_____

Day 5

Maybe you're a mom, a coworker, in ministry, a business partner, or a wife, and though you enjoy tending to the affairs of your life, you sometimes feel unnoticed, disregarded, or like what you do is never enough. I want to tell you that you're not alone. We have all struggled with feeling taken for granted. So what are you to do if your husband is not the Proverbs 31 man who praises you and calls you blessed? What if it feels like the only reason anyone is calling you is to get your attention so you can meet more of their needs?

Every morning before my kids head to school, I speak this blessing drawn from Isaiah 43:4 over them: "You are loved. You are known. You are precious in His sight." One day, as I was saying this to my last child at morning drop-off, the words echoed in my own heart: *You are loved. You are known. You are precious in His sight.*

Do you hear God's blessing over you? You may not have a husband or children rising up to call you blessed, but the Lord sings over you with words of truth: *You are loved. You are known. You are precious in My sight.*

You may suffer, as I do, from spiritual amnesia. In the midst of life's menial tasks, it's easy to lose sight of whom we are serving. That's when we need to go back to our source of truth. In Colossians 3:23, Paul says, "Whatever you do, work at it with all your heart, as working for the Lord, not for men."

Let's lean into our identity as God intended. In light of who we are in Christ, we live differently but not perfectly. The Spirit helps us in our weakness (Romans 8:26) to speak life-giving words, steward our time in a way that honors Him, and seek God's approval, not man's.

Have you ever felt like you're taken for granted or your work is not appreciated? Take this to God and ask Him to comfort you.

_____

_____

_____

_____

_____

Day 6

There are many places in Paul's letter to the Ephesians that tell us who we are in Christ. Our confidence lies in what He says about us, not in the approval of others. Let's take a look at what Ephesians 1:3–8 says:

→ We are blessed with every spiritual blessing in Christ.
→ He chose us in Him before the creation of the world to be holy and blameless.
→ In love we were adopted.
→ In Him we have redemption.
→ He lavishes us with His grace.

In Ephesians 5:1–2, we are told that we are God's "dearly loved children," who should therefore "follow God's example" and "walk in the way of love, just as Christ loved us and gave himself up for us." My dear sisters, I echo the words of Paul in Ephesians 4:1: "I urge you to live a life worthy of the calling you have received."

Because you are a daughter of the King, you walk in that manner. Because we are adopted children of God, He has given our lives purpose. We can trust our good Father.

How does knowing these blessings give you purpose? What are some ways you can live differently in light of your identity in Christ?

_____

_____

_____

_____

_____

_____

_____

_____

_____

Day 7

It's the end of week six! Let's take some extra time today to review what we've learned and plan for the week ahead.

Review

Here's what we discussed this week.

→ Wisdom is not simply intellectual knowledge; it's interwoven into every aspect of your life.

→ No one can live out the character traits of Proverbs 31 on their own strength. No one can live them out perfectly, either. So we must lean into the work of Jesus Christ on the cross and what we've been given as His children.

→ The enemy is cunning, so our distractions and idleness can be disguised in busyness, social media, news updates, fear, text messages, and noise.

→ Because He is our Heavenly Father, we don't eat the bread of idleness. As daughters of the King, we have purpose.

→ You may not have a husband or children rising up to call you blessed, but the Lord sings over you with words of truth: *You are loved. You are known. You are precious in My sight.*

Answer these questions on your own or in a group.

1. What is one distraction in your life right now? What would your life look like today if you removed that distraction?

_____

_____

_____

_____

_____

_____

_____

_____

2. Think of those in your circle of influence who are most affected by the words you say. Would they say your words are wise and kind?

_____

_____

_____

_____

_____

_____

_____

_____

_____

_____

3. What is a verse you can bring to mind to remind yourself to seek God's approval rather than that of other people? If you don't already have a favorite, try out Matthew 6:33.

_____

_____

_____

_____

_____

_____

_____

_____

_____

4. This week or today, how did you approach God? Complete the following sentence: God, I approach You believing You are _____ (distant, loving, angry, gracious, etc.).

_____

_____

_____

_____

_____

_____

_____

_____

5. This week, when did you feel far from God? Think of a moment of regret, discouragement, anxiety, or fear, and write it below. Then, instead of holding on to it, release it to the Lord. Ask for forgiveness, if needed, and receive His comfort and grace.

_____

_____

_____

_____

_____

_____

_____

_____

_____

Act

Here are some things you can do in the next week to put the lessons you've learned into action.

→ Practice intention with your speech. Ask yourself, "Is what I'm about to say wise? Is it kind?"

→ When you find yourself frustrated by a difficult or boring task, turn it into a note of gratitude.

→ When our Heavenly Father looks at His children, He sees us through His Son. Write the following words paraphrased from Isaiah 43:4 on a notecard: "You are loved. You are known. You are precious in His sight." Place the card on your bathroom mirror or somewhere else you can read it regularly.

Week Seven

Charm is deceptive, and beauty is fleeting;
but a woman who fears the Lord is to be praised.
Honor her for all that her hands have done,
and let her works bring her praise
at the city gate.

PROVERBS 31:30–31

Day 1

Remember way back in the "How to Use This Book" section when we talked about how Proverbs 31 is an acrostic poem that starts each line with a letter from the Hebrew alphabet? You may recall that John Piper described this as "stringing pearls," pulling together ideas to make a beautiful image rather than constructing an argument. So let's "string the pearls" as we recall what we have learned over the past few weeks.

In the first week, we discussed how Proverbs 31 is not a list of accomplishments to be checked off, and no matter how many virtues we display or good works we perform, it's ultimately our faith in Jesus that saves us.

In the second week, we talked about how God's never-ending love allows us to let go of our fears and serve joyfully.

The third week, we were reminded that He is the God who sees, so you can surrender the work of your hands to Him, no matter how dire your circumstances are.

In the fourth week, we saw God's gracious provision for His people, which allows us to be fearless and generous women of valor.

The fifth week, we talked about His faithfulness, which reminds us to be confident and hopeful women in the Lord.

In the sixth week, we unfolded our blessings as daughters of the King. We don't eat the bread of idleness because, in Him, we have purpose.

Finally, in week seven, we will learn that because He is God Almighty, we can be God-fearing and, on the flip side, not to fear anything *but* God.

The Bible is filled with countless stories of men and women who fear the Lord. In fact, some form of the word *yare*, which is Hebrew for "fear," is used hundreds of times in the Bible—including Proverbs 31:30. But *yare* doesn't just mean "fear"; it also means "awe" and "reverence." It's the kind of fear that draws us nearer to God, not further away. I think of it as similar to a loving relationship between a child and their parents: The child doesn't live in fear of their parents, but when they act disobedient, they have a healthy fear of discipline. As children of God, we have nothing to be afraid of, for nothing can separate us from His love. But we should have a healthy fear of His wrath as it impacts our lives.

Day 2

So, what does it look like to fear the Lord? Let's take a look at a few examples from the Bible.

Exodus 1:17 Pharaoh commanded the midwives to kill the Hebrew baby boys. "The midwives, however, feared God" and "let the boys live."

Proverbs 1:7 "The fear of the Lord is the beginning of knowledge."

Haggai 1:12 The people "obeyed the voice of the Lord their God" because they "feared the Lord."

Proverbs 8:13 "To fear the Lord is to hate evil."

Jeremiah 10:24–25 Jeremiah told those who disobeyed God that not fearing the Lord had "deprived [them] of good."

Proverbs 14:26 "Whoever fears the Lord has a secure fortress, and for their children it will be a refuge."

Guided Prayer

Heavenly Father, I come before You and praise You because You do not look at our outward appearances but at our hearts. I acknowledge that I do not always fear You; sometimes, instead, I fear people. I find my worth and value in what people have to say. Teach me to fear You, Lord! Fear draws me closer to You, as I realize You are God and I am not. This fear gives me confidence, contentment, and wisdom, and it prospers me. Help me see Your mighty hand at work in me and through me, in spite of me. Lord, I am in awe of You! In Your name I pray, amen.

Day 3

The Bible does tell us who we are and what we should do, but it does so through the lens of who God is. The knowledge of God and the knowledge of self always go hand in hand.

—JEN WILKIN

A woman who fears the Lord has her eyes fixed on Jesus. We are transformed to be more like Him when we gaze upon Him. This gazing and faithfully seeking Him is what changes us from the inside out. In the midst of your day-to-day tasks, do you ever find yourself consumed by earthly things rather than things above? Are you feeding your mind with things that are fleeting? The things we fill our minds with affect how we view God, ourselves, and the world around us. Take a moment to confess it to Him and ask Him to "set your mind on things above, not on earthly things" (Colossians 3:2).

Ponder for a moment where you're setting your gaze. Spend some time evaluating whether you're seeking after God's heart or other people's by looking at where you're spending your time. Make a list of five things that take up your time. Then pray and ask God to show you which ones are not helping you gaze on Jesus and ask Him to help you remove them.

1. _____

_____

_____

_____

2. _____

_____

_____

_____

3. _____

_____

_____

_____

4. _____

_____

_____

_____

5. _____

_____

_____

_____

Day 4

As women, we are constantly bombarded with lies about charm and beauty from the enemy, our own insecurity, and constant comparison with other women. We are told that, in order to find or keep a man, we must focus on our physical beauty and outward adornment. The enemy is pleased when we spend all of our energy on things that are here today but gone tomorrow.

Now, don't get me wrong; there's nothing wrong with taking care of your appearance. But what I'm saying is that it shouldn't be your focus or the thing from which you derive your identity. Do not let the enemy fool you into believing that your beauty, outward adornment, or successes in life are all that you have to offer this world, your family, your community, or a man. "For everything in the world—the lust of the flesh, the lust of the eyes, and the pride of life—comes not from the Father but from the world. The world and its desires pass away, but whoever does the will of God lives forever" (1 John 2:16–17). We are women who fear the Lord when we set our gaze and affections on Him.

What would it look like for you to set your mind on things above this week? What specific actions can you take? What can you tell yourself to refocus your affections and identity on Him?

_____

_____

_____

_____

_____

_____

_____

_____

_____

_____

Day 5

Throughout this study, we've talked about different attributes of God and what they mean for our lives. Thinking about everything you've read over the past seven weeks, fill in the blanks below. There are no right or wrong answers.

Because God is my Savior, I can be

_____

Because God is loving, I can joyfully

_____

Because He is the God who sees, I can surrender

_____

Because God provides, I can be

_____

Because He is faithful, I am

_____

Because He is my Heavenly Father, I have

_____

Because He is Almighty, I am

_____

1. What attribute of God have you become more thankful
    for this week?

    _____

    _____

    _____

    _____

    _____

    _____

    _____

    _____

    _____

2. Conversely, what characteristic or attribute of God has been
    challenging for you to embrace?

    _____

    _____

    _____

    _____

    _____

_____

_____

_____

_____

3. Sit for a moment and ask God to show you why it's been chal-
    lenging, then ask Him to make that character or attribute of
    Himself more present and real in your life this week.

_____

_____

_____

_____

_____

_____

_____

_____

_____

Day 6

When we left the mission field in Ecuador, our family grieved the loss of that beautiful country and the community that we had come to call "framily"—friends who had become like family. But in the midst of reacclimating to life in the United States, we discovered so many new things that we really enjoyed. Shortly after our arrival back in America, I found my son overwhelmed with the loss of friendships and rhythms of life he had been used to. So I introduced to him what I call "the power of 'and.'" I told him, "I know you're sad that your friends from Ecuador aren't a part of your life anymore—*and* you're excited about the new friends you're making. Both are possible. They can exist alongside each other."

As we come to the last verse of Proverbs 31, I want us to embrace the power of "and." At first glance, it may seem like verses 30 and 31 have nothing to do with each other. One is focusing on nurturing our faith and hearts, while the other is focused on what we do. But when you look closer, these verses are inseparable from each other. We are called to be women who cultivate God-fearing faith, not just the work of our hands—*and* God honors the work of our hands when it comes from a heart that fears the Lord.

This life-giving poem ends with praise and honor for the work of your hands and your God-fearing heart. Sister in Christ, this is God cheering you on for being a woman of valor who fears the Lord. This is God singing praise over you because He is the God who sees the struggles, the challenges, and the menial tasks that have to be performed day in and out. He sees the long hours you clock at work. He sees your desire to honor him in your relationships. He sees you get up in the middle of the night to slay monsters under beds and hold fearful hearts. He sees you show up each morning, even when everything inside you wants to hide under the covers. He sees you listen with compassion to that person who needs a listening ear. He sees you fervently pray for your loved ones. My dear sisters, never doubt His promises; you can always trust His word. "This is what the Lord says, he who created you . . . he who formed you . . . 'Do not fear, for I have redeemed you; I have summoned you by name; you are mine'" (Isaiah 43:1).

I pray this study has opened the eyes of your heart to see Him more clearly and deepened your trust and love for Him. May the reminders that you're a daughter of the King echo in your heart.

Day 7

Congratulations! You've reached the end of this Bible study. Let's have one last longer study session to draw these seven weeks to a close.

Review

Here's what we talked about this week.

→ This passage praises not just any kind of woman but a godly woman who fears the Lord.

→ Fearing God Almighty draws us nearer to Him, not further away. A healthy fear of God's discipline is different from being afraid of God. As children of God, we have nothing to be afraid of, for nothing can separate us from His love.

→ The enemy is pleased when we spend all of our energy on things that are here today but gone tomorrow, like fleeting charm and physical beauty.

→ We are called to be women who focus on our hearts *and* the fruit that comes from the work of our hands.

→ A woman who fears the Lord has her eyes fixed on Jesus. This gazing and faithfully seeking Him is what changes us from the inside out.

Answer these questions on your own or in a group.

1. What is keeping you from developing godly virtues in your life?

_____

_____

_____

_____

_____

_____

_____

_____

_____

2. What is encouraging you to develop godly virtues in your life?

_____

_____

_____

_____

_____

_____

_____

_____

_____

_____

3. Write down two truths you've learned (or relearned) during this Bible study.

_____

_____

_____

_____

_____

_____

_____

_____

_____

4. Write down one thing you want to work on this week.

_____

_____

_____

_____

_____

_____

_____

_____

_____

_____

5. Write out a prayer to God based on the two truths you learned and the one thing you want to work on.

_____

_____

_____

_____

_____

_____

_____

_____

_____

Act

Here are some things you can do to put the lessons of this book into action.

→ Share with someone in your life two things God has been teaching you through this study.

→ Honor someone this week for what they do for those around them, no matter how small an act.

→ Memorize Proverbs 31:30.

→ Recommit yourself to fixing your eyes on Jesus.

Moving Forward

You may have started this study asking a common question: "How am I supposed to accomplish everything that the Proverbs 31 woman does?" But if we only look at her accomplishments, we miss what this passage has to tell us. Hopefully, as this study unfolded, you started asking, "How can I know and trust God more like the Proverbs 31 woman does? How can I offer the ordinary, everyday tasks of my life to Him?" Because when you get to know God, really know Him, He changes you. Even the mundane is transformed. Spending time at His feet and fervently seeking Him in prayer changes our hearts and fills us with hope, confidence, strength, courage, boldness, and audacity.

I hope you have fallen in love with Jesus in a deeper way over the past seven weeks and discovered the freedom that comes with knowing who He is so you can use the influence He's given you right where you are. My prayer is that you were challenged each week to be a woman of valor who trusts in God and abides in His truth.

You are a Proverbs 31 woman when you're connecting to His heart and allowing the redeeming work of the cross into the crevices of your soul. In Christ we are daughters of the King—chosen, loved, more than conquerors, wise, redeemed, and forgiven. But we're also prone to spiritual amnesia, and we need to constantly lean into His Spirit for guidance and grace.

By now, you know that Proverbs 31 is not an exhortation or command to do or be but a declaration of who you are. We are women of valor because God dwells in us and loves through us. His transformative power on the cross works in us. This is what happens when we know our God's truth is being lived out in us through the power of the Holy Spirit.

I leave you with the words of an amazing woman of valor, Mother Teresa: "Love begins at home, and it is not how much we do, but how much love we put in the action that we do." I challenge you, as a woman of valor, to put His love into action as you navigate the influence God has given you and use it for His glory.

References

Akin, Daniel. "Darlene Diebler Rose: Unwavering Faith in God's Promises." International Mission Board. Accessed May 2, 2020. https://www.imb.org/2017/05/10/darlenedieblerrose/.

Barton, Ruth Haley. *Sacred Rhythms: Arranging Our Lives for Spiritual Transformation*. Downers Grove: InterVarsity Press, 2006.

Bojaxhiu, Mary Teresa. "Nobel Lecture." Lecture presented in Oslo, Norway, December 11, 1979. Accessed May 2, 2020. https://www.nobelprize.org/prizes/peace/1979/teresa /lecture/.

Covey, Stephen. *The 7 Habits of Highly Effective People: Powerful Lessons in Personal Change*. New York: Free Press, 2004.

Cunnion, Jeannie. *Mom Set Free: Find Relief from the Pressure to Get It All Right*. Brentwood: Howard Books, 2017.

Eller, Suzanne. *The Spirit-Led Heart: Living a Life of Love and Faith without Borders*. Bloomington: Bethany House, 2018.

Freeman, Emily. *Grace for the Good Girl: Letting Go of the Try-Hard Life*. Ada: Revell, 2011.

Giglio, Louie. *Waiting Here for You: An Advent Journey of Hope*. Nashville: Thomas Nelson, 2015.

Graham, Billy. *Hope for Each Day: Words of Wisdom and Faith*. Nashville: Thomas Nelson, 2017.

Krauszer, Michael. "What Does the Color Purple Mean or Symbolize in the Bible." *Christian Crier* (blog). October 31, 2014. https:// www.patheos.com/blogs/christiancrier/2014/10/31/what -does-the-color-purple-mean-or-symbolize-in-the-bible/.

Manning, Brennan. *The Ragamuffin Gospel: Good News for the Bedraggled, Beat-Up, and Burnt Out*. New York: Multnomah, 2008.

Piper, John. "Put on the Lord Jesus Christ, Part 1." Desiring God. Accessed May 2, 2020. https://www.desiringgod.org /messages/put-on-the-lord-jesus-christ-part-1.

Piper, John. "A Woman Who Fears the Lord Is to Be Praised: Mother's Day." Desiring God. Accessed May 2, 2020. https://www.desiringgod.org/messages/a-woman-who -fears-the-lord-is-to-be-praised.

Pulliam, Elisa. *Unblinded Faith: Gaining Spiritual Sight Through Believing God's Word*. Eugene: Harvest House, 2018.

Tada, Joni Eareckson. *A Place of Healing: Wrestling with the Mysteries of Suffering, Pain, and God's Sovereignty*. Colorado Springs: David C. Cook, 2015.

Wilkin, Jen. *Women of the Word: How to Study the Bible with Both Our Hearts and Our Minds*. Wheaton: Crossway, 2014.

Index

M

Mary and Martha, 32
Matthew 6:33, 132
Matthew 7:11, 88
Matthew 20:28, 45
Menial tasks, 124, 126, 152
Moses, 106, 108
Mother Teresa, 161

N

Noah, 72
Noble character, 2, 4, 18

P

Parks, Rosa, 64
Paul (apostle), *x*, 2, 93, 101, 126, 128
Personality types, 96
1 Peter 2:9, 22
Pharaoh, 140
Philippians 2:12–13, 52
Philippians 4:12, 93
Piper, John, *x*, 100, 138
Prayer, 17, 37, 59, 79, 99, 119, 141
Proverbs 1:7, 140
Proverbs 8:13, 140
Proverbs 14:26, 140
Proverbs 31, *ix*, 160
  acrostic poem, *x*, 138
  celebration of women, 64
  character traits in, 41, 96, 108, 130
  life-giving poem, 152
  as seasons in a woman's life, 6
  verse(s) 10–12, 1
  verse(s) 13–15, 25
  verse(s) 10–31, *xii–xiii*, 64
  verse(s) 16–19, 51, 64
  verse(s) 20–22, 71, 74
  verse 23, 109
  verse(s) 23–25, 95
  verse 25, 102
  verse(s) 26–29, 115
  verse 27, 120
  verse 30, 139, 158
  verse(s) 30–31, 137

Proverbs 31 woman, *ix*, 160
  character building, 52
  godly virtues of, 62, 101
  identity of, 38
  opening hands to others, 80
  providing things of value, 26
  strength of, 60
  trusting in God, 79
  wisdom of, 116
  woman using her influence, 12, 41
Psalm 16, 104
Psalm 46:1, 10
Psalm 84:11, 79
Psalm 139:1–5, 69
Pulliam, Elisa, 78

Q

Queen Esther, 106, 108

R

Release and receive, season of, 38
Resilience, 57, 64
Resurrection, 56
Romans 8:26, 127
Romans 8:37, 2, 10
Romans 8:38, 37
Romans 10:9, 22
Romans 13:14, 101
Rose, Darlene D., 60–61, 64

S

Salvation, 2, 79
  Cross and, 16
  as gift, 22, 52
Sarah, Hagar and, 62
Satan
  how he speaks, 9
  lies of, 10, 88
  words of, 8
Savior, hope in, 2–3
Seasons of life, 8, 26, 52–53, 96, 99, 101
Service, 26–27, 37, 44, 45, 46
  motivation for, 28–29

Acknowledgments

To my husband and children: You inspire me to lean into Jesus and live out my faith. To my husband: In the midst of a global pandemic, you not only took charge of our boys' home education as you did your own job from home, but you also made dinner so I could meet my deadlines for this book. This book would not exist without your support and encouragement. I love you!

To my friends, mentors, teachers, pastors, and family who have poured into my life with love, grace, and truth: I am forever thankful for your wisdom and friendship.

Finally, to my gracious heavenly Father: Thank you for not giving up on me and persistently pursuing my heart. I'm in awe that You use me, in spite of me.

About the Author

 **Mari Hernandez-Tuten** loves to share God's truth and hope with women through mentoring, Bible teaching, family life coaching, and counseling. She's been in ministry for more than 20 years and has taught women from all over the world, leading seminars and workshops that encourage women and moms to lean into God's grace and truth. She's been on television and radio programs and has written hundreds of articles on family discipleship, parenting, and developing faith habits. You can connect with Mari at InspiredbyFamilyMag.com, where she writes about family, faith, feasting, and fun.

CPSIA information can be obtained
at www.ICGtesting.com
Printed in the USA
JSHW021923041021
19293JS00002B/3